Currency Conversion Tables

A hundred years of change

R. L. BIDWELL

Rex Collings
London
1970

Published by Rex Collings Ltd
42/44 Hanway Street
London W1

SBN 9017 2008 9

Printed in the Republic of Ireland
by Hely Thom Limited Dublin

CONTENTS

INTRODUCTION

During some recent historical research, nearly all the figures that I encountered were in French francs and Spanish pesetas. These I wished to convert into sterling so as to have some rough basis of reference as to their significance. Does, for example, a salary of 600 francs a month in 1921 seem a good wage or a miserly one? As can be seen from pages 19–21 the rate of exchange between the franc and the pound sterling has varied between 25.1 and 1374. To find out the rate in any particular year I had to go to daily newspapers or other sources. Finally, to save myself trouble, I compiled a table of exchange rates for the period in which I was interested. It occurred to me that what I had found helpful might also be of use to other research workers in the fields of history, economics, sociology etc. I have therefore added to my original franc and peseta tables others covering the principal European currencies, those of South America and that of Japan. At the same time I have given the equivalent value of the various currencies in American dollars.

These tables aim to do no more than to give a rough answer to the question 'About how much was a – worth in 19–?'. They make no attempt at scientific precision, for which a researcher would have to go to other sources. Rates of exchange vary daily and often according to the type of transaction. There is a different rate for buying and selling, for banknotes and travellers' cheques, for spot and forward dealings.

A further factor means that many of the figures given can only be approximate. Exchange control was introduced in Latin America and some of the Balkan countries in the thirties. A system of bonuses and premiums makes exact calculation impossible. Exchange control was extended to many other countries after 1945. In Latin America, in particular, there was very little resemblance between the official rate, the recognized 'free' rate and the black market rate.

The price of gold on the London bullion market is given as some indication of the declining value of the £ sterling. Otherwise no account is taken of the decline in the actual amount of goods – say ounces of gin – that could be bought for £1 at any particular time.

I should like to thank the Librarian and staff of the Marshall Library at Cambridge for their kindness and help in finding answers to the problems that I met while compiling these tables. Naturally, no one except myself is responsible for any mistakes that may be found.

UNITED STATES
CANADA

100 cents — 1 dollar

	$ (US) TO £1	$ (CANADIAN) TO £1
Pre–war parity	4.867	4.867
1915 – Jan	4.86	4.86
1916 – Jan	4.77	4.77
1917 – Jan	4.76	4.79
1918 – Jan	4.76	4.8
1919 – Jan	4.76	4.85
Jun	4.61	4.5
Aug	4.3	4.35
Nov	4.03	4.25
1920 – Jan	3.7	4.02
Jun	3.95	4.5
Oct	3.5	3.85
1921 – Jan	3.8	4.3
1922 – Jan	4.2	4.4
Jun	4.5	4.5
1923 – Jan	4.65	4.68
1924 – Jan	4.25	4.35
1925 – Jan	4.74	4.78
1926 – Jan	4.85	4.85
1927 – Jan	4.85	4.85
1928 – Jan	4.87	4.88
1929 – Jan	4.85	4.86
1930 – Jan	4.87	4.93
1931 – Jan	4.87	4.86
Oct	3.9	4.5
1932 – Jan	3.38	4.0
1933 – Jan	3.34	3.8
Jun	4.05	4.53

	$ (US) TO £1	$ (CANADIAN) TO £1
1933 – Oct	4.5	4.7
1934 – Jan	5.0	5.0
1935 – Jan	4.93	4.89
1936 – Jan	4.93	4.94
1937 – Jan	4.91	4.90
1938 – Jan	5.0	5.0
1939 – Jan	4.63	4.67
1940 – Jan	4.03	4.04
1941 – average	4.03	4.92
1942 – average	4.03	4.45
1943 – average	4.03	4.45
1944 – average	4.03	4.45
1945 – average	4.03	4.45
1946 – average	4.03	4.24
1947 – average	4.03	4.03
1948 – average	4.03	4.03
1949 – Jan	4.03	4.03
Oct	2.80	3.08
1950 – average	2.80	3.04
1951 – average	2.80	2.95
1952 – average	2.79	2.73
1953 – average	2.81	2.77
1954 – average	2.81	2.73
1955 – average	2.79	2.75
1956 – average	2.80	2.75
1957 – average	2.79	2.68
1958 – average	2.81	2.73
1959 – average	2.81	2.69
1960 – average	2.81	2.72
1961 – average	2.81	2.84
1962 – Jan	2.81	2.95
May	2.81	3.03
1963 – average	2.80	3.02

	$ (US) TO £1	$ (CANADIAN) TO £1
1964 – average	2.79	3.01
1965 – average	2.80	3.01
1966 – average	2.79	3.01
1967 – Jan	2.79	3.01
Nov	2.41	2.6
1968 – average	2.4	2.6
1969 – average	2.4	2.6

AUSTRIA

Before 1898 100 kreuzer – 1 gulder or florin. There were 10.2 florins to £1 and 2 to $1. From 1898 100 heller – 1 krone

	KRONE TO £1	KRONE TO $1
Pre-war parity	24.02	4.935
1916 – Jan	—	7.60
1917 – Jan	—	8.60
1919 – May	110	23.2
Aug	170	38.5
Sep	190 – 270	42 – 68
Nov	400 – 500	99 – 130
1920 – Jan	690 – 960	180 – 260
Jun	580 – 610	140 – 150
Oct	940 – 1400	270 – 405
Dec	1785 – 2350	513 – 670
1921 – Jan	2352 – 3130	670 – 786
Jun	2325 – 2720	610 – 727
Sep	4115 – 9600	1103 – 2585
Nov	18,000 – 34,500	4600 – 8600
1922 – Jan	24,550 – 43,800	5825 – 10,200
Jun	50,325 – 84,400	11,250 – 19,025
Aug	226,000 – 346,000	51,075 – 77,600
Oct	325,000 – 330,000	73,800 – 74,300
1923 – Jan	310,000 – 350,000	66,700 – 75,300
Jun	315,000 – 335,000	67,750 – 72,004
1924 – Jan	300,000	70,600
Jun	306,000	70,500
1925 – Jan	338,000	79,700

New currency introduced — 100 groschen – 1 schilling

	SCHILLING TO £1	SCHILLING TO $1
1925 – May	34.4	7.08
1926 – Jan	34.4	7.08
1927 – Jan	34.4	7.08
1928 – Jan	34.4	7.08
1929 – Jan	34.5	7.11
1930 – Jan	34.5	7.11
1931 – Jan	34.5	7.11
Oct	30	7.7
1932 – Jan	30	8.93
1933 – Jan	28.5	8.57
1934 – Jan	30	6.0
1935 – Jan	26.5	5.40
1936 – Jan	26.5	5.40
1937 – Jan	26.5	5.38
1945 – autumn	40	10 *(Military rate)*
1946 – Dec	40	10.14 *(First official quotation)*
1949 – Nov	*Three official rates were introduced which varied according to the type of transaction:*	
	40.32	14.03
	59.8	21.36
	72.8	26.0
	These continued until	
1950 – Oct	*when only two rates were official:*	
	59.8	21.49
	72.8	26.13
	These continued until a single rate was introduced	
1953 – May	72.8	26.08
1954 – average	73.02	26.08

	SCHILLING TO £1	SCHILLING TO $1
1955 – average	73.02	26
1956 – average	73.02	26
1957 – average	72.66	26
1958 – average	72.5	26
1959 – average	72.7	26
1960 – average	72.9	26
1961 – average	72.65	26
1962 – average	72.5	25.82
1963 – average	72.31	25.83
1964 – average	72.2	25.83
1965 – average	72.2	25.83
1966 – average	72.2	25.83
1967 – Jan	72.2	25.83
Nov	62.32	25.83
1968 – average	61.71	25.88
1969 – average	61.7	25.89

BELGIUM

100 centimes – 1 franc (from 1927–1940 exchange rates were usually quoted in Belgas *of 5 francs. For simplicity franc figures are retained for this period)*

	FRANCS TO £1	FRANCS TO $1
Pre-war parity	25.221	5.183
1914 – Jan	25.4	5.2
1919 – Jan	27	5.77
Jun	30.8	6.65
Oct	36	8.6
1920 – Jan	43.25	11.65
Apr	60	16.12
Jun	45.5	11.5
Oct	50.5	14.55
1921 – Jan	57.1	16.08
Apr	53	13.45
Oct	55	13.91
1922 – Jan	55	13.15
Sep	61.5	13.82
Dec	70.3	15.11
1923 – Jan	68.0 – 91.8	14.62 – 19.74
Jun	82.2 – 89.0	17.67 – 19.14
Oct	85.0 – 92.95	18.80 – 20.52
1924 – Jan	96.2 – 106.25	22.64 – 25.0
Jun	89.0 – 101.25	20.94 – 23.80
Oct	93	21.9
1925 – Jan	94.8	20
1926 – Jan	107	22.02
Apr	130	26.75
Aug	170	34.98
1927 – Jan	174.5	36.0

	FRANCS TO £1	FRANCS TO $1
1928 – Jan	174.5	36.0
1929 – Jan	174.5	36.0
1930 – Jan	174.5	36.0
1931 – Jan	173.8	36.0
Oct	140	35.9
1932 – Jan	121.25	36.0
1933 – Jan	121.25	36.0
1934 – Jan	117	23.4
1935 – Jan	105	21.3
Apr	140	28.87 *Devalued*
1936 – Jan	146.5	29.56
1937 – Jan	145.4	29.63
1938 – Jan	147	29.59
1939 – Jan	137.5	29.68
1940 – Jan	120	29.63
1945 – average	176.6	43.96
1946 – average	176.6	43.96
1947 – average	176.6	43.96
1948 – average	176.6	43.96
1949 – Jan	176.6	43.96
Oct	140	50.15 *Devalued*
1950 – average	140	50.0
1951 – average	140	50.4
1952 – average	140	50.5
1953 – average	139.7	50.19
1954 – average	139.4	50.0
1955 – average	139.6	50.0
1956 – average	140.4	49.88
1957 – average	139.75	50.2
1958 – average	139.7	49.9
1959 – average	139.8	49.9
1960 – average	139.3	49.7

	FRANCS TO £1	FRANCS TO $1
1961 – average	139.7	49.8
1962 – average	139.4	49.7
1963 – average	139.36	49.84
1964 – average	138.46	49.72
1965 – average	139.15	49.65
1966 – average	139.66	50.03
1967 – Jan	139.18	49.81
Nov	119.42	49.4
1968 – average	120	49.4
1969 – average	119.8	50

BULGARIA

100 stotinki – 1 leva (from 1878)

	LEVA TO £1	LEVA TO $1
Pre-war parity	25.221	5.183
1914 – Jan	28	5.76
1915 – Jan	31	6.38
1916 – Jan	33	6.96
1919 – Mar	60	14
Jun	88	19
Aug	116	27
Sep	152	35
1920 – Jan	165	40
May	240	58
Aug	180	49
Oct	225	63
1921 – Jan	280	78
Aug	360	99
Oct	470 – 540	126 – 138
Dec	527 – 600	125 – 150
1922 – Jan	558 – 620	133 – 147
Jun	579 – 650	133 – 150
Oct	669 – 723	149 – 166
1923 – Jan	630 – 800	135 – 172
Jun	325 – 525	70 – 113
Oct	440 – 500	99 – 110
1924 – Jan	570 – 625	134 – 147
1925 – Jan	645	136
1926 – Jan	675	138.89
1927 – Jan	675	138.89
1928 – Jan	675	138.89
1929 – Jan	669	138.43

	LEVA TO £1	LEVA TO $1
1930 – Jan	675	138.89
1931 – Jan	669	137.66
Oct	540	138.46
1932 – Jan	480	142.86
1933 – Jan	480	142.86
1934 – Jan	465	93
1935 – Jan	420	85.19
1936 – Jan	400	84.0
1937 – Jan	405	84.3
1938 – Jan	405	84.3
1939 – Jan	385	84.4
1940 – Jan	320	83.9
1946 – average	1158	290
	These rates continued until	
1949 – Nov	797	290
	The leva was then linked to the rouble and revalued	
1952 – May	19.04	6.80
	A special rate was given for some transactions	
1957 – Jul	26.6	9.52
	A new leva was then introduced	
1962 – Jan	3.2	1.17
	and there were later special rates	
	5.6	2
	These continued until the official rate was	
1967 – Nov	2.8	1.7
	4.8	2 *special rate*

CZECHOSLOVAKIA

100 haleru – 1 koruna (crown)

	CROWNS TO £1	CROWNS TO $1
1919 – official parity	24.02	4.93
Mar	75 – 81	14.7 – 16.2
Aug	91 – 99	19.0 – 23.0
Oct	126 – 161	29.0 – 35.0
1920 – Jan	222 – 283	52.0 – 79.5
Mar	287 – 337	74.5 – 98.5
Jun	181	45.5
Oct	261 – 328	74.5 – 88.8
1921 – Jan	283 – 328	74.0 – 91.5
Mar	300	76.0
Jun	272	72.0
Oct	353 – 419	90.5 – 104.0
1922 – Jan	219 – 277	52.2 – 66.5
Mar	233 – 270	53.2 – 62.0
Jun	231	52.4
Aug	123 – 183	27.5 – 41.0
Oct	125 – 140	28.4 – 31.5
1923 – Jan	160	34.4
1924 – Jan	147	34.6
1925 – Jan	158	33.33
1926 – Jan	164	33.74
1927 – Jan	164	33.74
1928 – Jan	164	33.74
1929 – Jan	164	33.74
1930 – Jan	164	33.74
1931 – Jan	164	33.74
Oct	134	34.36
1932 – Jan	114	33.93

	CROWNS TO £1	CROWNS TO $1
1933 – Jan	113	33.92
1934 – Jan	109	20.45
1935 – Jan	117	23.74
1936 – Jan	119	25.15
1937 – Jan	140	28.69
1938 – Jan	142	28.88
1939 – Jan	135	29.23
1945 – Oct	201	50
	These rates continued until	
1949 – Nov	140	50
	These rates continued until the introduction of a new crown	
1953 – Jun	20.16	7.2 *Official*
	40.32	14.4 *T/Cheques etc.*
	Apart from adjustment to the devaluation of £ sterling these have continued unchanged	
1967 – Nov	17.22	7.2 *Official*
	37.22	14.4 *T/Cheques etc.*

DENMARK

Before 1875 96 skilling – 1 rigsdaler. There were 9 rigsdalers to £1 and approximately 2 to \$1. After 1875 100 ore – 1 krone

	KRONE TO £1	KRONE TO \$1
1876	18.16	3.73
1914 – Jan	18.25	3.76
1915 – Jan	19.2	4.04
1916 – Jan	17.45	3.72
1917 – Jan	17.35	3.67
1918 – Jan	15.5	3.29
1919 – Jan	18.0	3.78
1920 – Jan	20.9	5.59
Aug	24.0	6.62
1921 – Jan	20.0	5.13
1922 – Jan	21.0	4.98
1923 – Jan	23.2	4.99
1924 – Jan	25.2	5.93
1925 – Jan	26.8	5.65
Jul	20.35	4.9
1926 – Jan	19.6	4.06
1927 – Jan	18.2	3.73
1928 – Jan	18.2	3.73
1929 – Jan	18.2	3.73
1930 – Jan	18.2	3.73
1931 – Jan	18.2	3.73
Oct	18.0	4.62
1932 – Jan	18.0	5.36
1933 – Jan	19.3	5.74
1934 – Jan	22.4	4.8
1935 – Jan	22.4	4.52
1936 – Jan	22.4	4.52

	KRONE TO £1	KRONE TO $1
1937 – Jan	22.4	4.54
1938 – Jan	22.4	4.60
1939 – Jan	22.4	4.92
1940 – Jan	20.5	5.18
1945 – average	19.34	4.80
1946 – average	19.34	4.81
1947 – average	19.34	4.81
1948 – average	19.34	4.81
1949 – Jan	19.34	4.8
Oct	19.34	6.9 *Devalued*
1950 – average	19.34	6.9
1951 – average	19.34	6.9
1952 – average	19.34	6.9
1953 – average	19.34	6.9
1954 – average	19.41	6.9
1955 – average	19.36	6.9
1956 – average	19.36	6.9
1957 – average	19.4	6.9
1958 – average	19.35	6.9
1959 – average	19.35	6.9
1960 – average	19.35	6.9
1961 – average	19.35	6.9
1962 – average	19.35	6.9
1963 – average	19.35	6.9
1964 – average	19.35	6.9
1965 – average	19.35	6.9
1966 – average	19.35	6.9
1967 – Jan	19.35	6.9
Nov	18.01	7.5
1968 – average	18.0	7.5
1969 – average	17.9	7.5

FINLAND

100 penni – 1 markka

	MARKKA TO £1	MARKKA TO $1
1914 – Jan	25.5	5.23
1915 – Jan	29	6
1916 – Jan	35.5	7.6
1917 – Jan	35.5	7.6
1918 – Jan	32	7
1919 – Jan	43	9
Jul	53 – 77	11.95 – 17.70
Oct	84 – 101	20.1 – 24.7
1920 – Jan	86 – 125	24.8 – 33
Apr	72	18.3
Jul	93 – 103	23.8 – 27.7
Oct	121 – 156	34.9 – 45.0
1921 – Jan	111 – 125	29.5 – 35.25
Mar	135 – 159	35.0 – 40.5
Jun	192 – 253	49.75 – 66.75
Oct	243 – 261	62.25 – 70.25
1922 – Jan	211 – 228	49.75 – 54.0
Mar	205 – 218	47.5 – 50.0
Jun	193 – 210	44.0 – 47.25
Oct	180 – 200	40.55 – 45.55
1923 – Jan	186	40.0
1924 – Jan	171	40.24
1925 – Jan	188	39.67
1926 – Jan	192.5	39.71
1927 – Jan	192.8	39.81
1928 – Jan	193.5	39.71
1929 – Jan	192.5	39.71
1930 – Jan	194	40.0
1931 – Jan	193	40.0

	MARKKA TO £1	MARKKA TO $1	
1931 – Oct	160	41.03	
1932 – Jan	240	71.43	
1933 – Jan	227	67.56	
1934 – Jan	227	45.2	
1935 – Jan	227	45.82	
1936 – Jan	227	45.82	
1937 – Jan	227	46.06	
1938 – Jan	227	46.02	
1939 – Jan	227	48.26	
1940 – Jan	220	49.35	
1945 – May	196	44	
Jun	343	86.3	*Devalued*
Jul	485	120.8	*Devalued*
Oct	547	136	*Devalued*
1946 – average	547	136	
1947 – average	547	136	
1948 – average	547	136	
1949 – Jan	547	136	
Jul	646	160	*Devalued*
Oct	646	230	*Devalued*
1950 – average	643	230	
1951 – average	643	230	
1952 – average	643	230	
1953 – average	643	230	
1954 – average	643	230	
1955 – average	643	230	
1956 – average	643	230	
1957 – Jan	643	230	
Sep	896	320	*Devalued*
1958 – average	896	320	
1959 – average	896	320	
1960 – average	896	320	

	MARKKA TO £1	MARKKA TO $1
1961 – average	896	321.5
1962 – average	896	321.5
New currency introduced — 100 markke – 1 finnmark		
1963 – Jan	9	3.22
1964 – average	9	3.22
1965 – average	9	3.22
1966 – average	9	3.22
1967 – Jan	9	3.22
Oct	10	4.20 *Devalued*
1968 – average	10	4.20
1969 – average	10	4.20

FRANCE

100 centimes – 1 franc

	FRANCS TO £1	FRANCS TO $1
1870	25.1	4.98
Pre-war parity	25.22	5.18
1914 – Jan	25.3	5.19
1915 – Jan	25.12	5.24
Oct	27.5	5.90
1916 – Jan	28	5.90
1917 – Jan	27.8	5.86
1918 – Jan	27.18	5.72
1919 – Jan	26	5.47
Jun	30	6.48
Oct	36	8.62
1920 – Jan	40.9 – 46.5	10.75 – 13.19
Mar	48.5 – 58.1	14.25 – 14.97
Jun	50.5	12.96
Oct	53.5	15.3
1921 – Jan	53.8 – 61.5	13.9 – 17.1
Mar	55	14.11
Jun	46.6	12.36
Oct	52	13.75
1922 – Jan	51.4	12.15
Mar	48.5	11.2
Jun	50	11.19
Oct	60	13.5
1923 – Jan	62 – 80	13.33 – 17.20
Jun	72	15.65
1924 – Jan	84 – 98	19.76 – 23.06
Mar	76 – 120	17.67 – 27.91
Jun	77 – 89	17.11 – 19.78
Oct	86.5	19.22

	FRANCS TO £1	FRANCS TO $1
1925 – Jan	88	18.57
Jun	97 – 108	19.96 – 22.22
Oct	102 – 120	20.99 – 24.68
1926 – Jan	129.25	26.59
1927 – Jan	122	25.10
1928 – Jan	124	25.52
1929 – Jan	124	25.52
1930 – Jan	123.9	25.50
1931 – Jan	123.67	25.43
Oct	100	25.64
1932 – Jan	86	25.59
1933 – Jan	86	25.59
1934 – Jan	83	16.6
1935 – Jan	74.5	15.31
1936 – Jan	75	15.31
Sep	105	21.4 *Devalued*
1937 – Jan	105	21.43
Jul	128	26.12
1938 – Jan	147	29.4
Mar	165	31.0
1939 – Jan	176.5	39.8
1940 – Jan	176.5	43.8
1945 – average	203	49.72
1946 – average	480	119.3
1947 – average	480	119.3
1948 – Jan	864	214.7
Oct	1062	349
1949 – Jan	1093	350
Oct	980	350
1950 – average	980	350
1951 – average	979	349.95
1952 – average	981	349.95

	FRANCS TO £1	FRANCS TO $1
1953 – average	982	349.95
1954 – average	981	349.95
1955 – average	978	349.95
1956 – average	982	350
1957 – Jan	984	350
Aug	1117	420
1958 – average	1117	420
1959 – average	1374	490
1960 – Jan	13.74	4.90 *New Francs*
1961 – average	13.7	4.9
1962 – average	13.7	4.9
1963 – average	13.7	4.9
1964 – average	13.7	4.9
1965 – average	13.7	4.9
1966 – average	13.8	4.9
1967 – Jan	13.8	4.9
Oct	11.8	4.9
1968 – average	11.8	4.9
1969 – Jan	11.8	4.9
Aug	13.3	5.5 *Devalued*

GERMANY

In the early years after 1870 some of the States retained their own currencies. Figures quoted here are for the mark of 100 pfennigs

	MARKS TO £1	MARKS TO $1
Pre-war parity	20.429	4.198
1915 – Jan	–	4.59
1916 – Jan	–	5.36
1917 – Jan	–	5.53
1920 – Feb	340	100.5
Apr	240	60.5
Jun	160	40.25
Oct	240	70.45
1921 – Jan	215 – 262	57 – 74
Jun	245 – 280	63 – 75
Oct	463 – 712	124 – 180
1922 – Jan	790 – 862	186 – 201
Feb	873 – 1009	204 – 227
Mar	1022 – 1485	230 – 338
Jul	1770 – 2975	402 – 670
Aug	2860 – 8850	644 – 1975
Oct	7925 – 20,350	1815 – 4500
Dec	31,000 – 39,000	6750 – 8470
1923 – Jan	32,000 – 225,000	6890 – 48,390
Jun	265,000 – 900,000	57,000 – 193,500
Aug	4.5 million – 52 million	900,000 – 11.4 million
Oct	1 milliard – 800 milliard	250 million – 170 milliard
Dec	15 billion – 25 billion	3.43 billion – 5.72 billion
1924 – Jan	19 billion	4.47 billion
	New currency introduced	
1925 – Jan	20	4.22

	MARKS TO £1	MARKS TO $1
1926 – Jan	20.3	4.18
1927 – Jan	20.4	4.2
1928 – Jan	20.45	4.21
1929 – Jan	20.4	4.20
1930 – Jan	20.4	4.20
1931 – Jan	20.4	4.20
Oct	17	4.36
1932 – Jan	14.25	4.24
1933 – Jan	14.10	4.2
1934 – Jan	13.6	2.61
1935 – Jan	12.1	2.45
1936 – Jan	12.25	2.48
1937 – Jan	12.25	2.48
1938 – Jan	12.4	2.49
1939 – Jan	11.5	2.49
1940 – Jan	–	2.5

The Allies in 1945 introduced a military rate of 40 marks to £1 and 10 to $1. This continued until the currency reform and the introduction of the Deutschmark

1948 – Jun	13.4	3.33
1949 – Jan	13.4	3.33
Sep	11.76	4.2 *Devalued*
1950 – average	11.76	4.2
1951 – average	11.76	4.2
1952 – average	11.5	4.2
1953 – average	11.70	4.2
1954 – average	11.73	4.2
1955 – average	11.74	4.2
1956 – average	11.71	4.2
1957 – average	11.73	4.2
1958 – average	11.72	4.2
1959 – average	11.74	4.18

	MARKS TO £1	MARKS TO $1
1960 – average	11.71	4.17
1961 – average	11.17	3.99
1962 – average	11.20	3.99
1963 – average	11.11	3.97
1964 – average	11.09	3.97
1965 – average	11.22	4.0
1966 – average	11.09	3.97
1967 – Jan	11.22	4.01
Oct	9.63	3.99
1968 – average	9.5	3.98
1969 – Jan	9.58	4.01
Oct	8.83	3.66 Revalued

GREECE

100 lepta – 1 drachma

	DRACHMA TO £1	DRACHMA TO $1
Pre-war parity	25.221	5.183
1919 – Jan	24.81	5.19
1920 – Jan	25.40	6.89
Mar	34.60	9.21
Oct	35	10.25
1921 – Jan	53	13.91
Jun	64	17.0
Oct	89	22.52
1922 – Jan	97	23.0
Jun	105	23.85
Aug	140	31.31
Oct	175 – 292	39.5 – 65.5
Dec	380	81.63
1923 – Jan	380	81.63
Jun	150	31.25
Oct	310	63.79
1924 – Jan	220	51.76
Oct	260	54.9
1925 – Jan	270	56.97
Jun	300	61.73
Oct	350	72.02
1926 – Jan	375	77.10
1927 – Jan	383	78.81
1928 – Jan	368	75.72
1929 – Jan	375	77.06
1930 – Jan	375	77.06
1931 – Jan	375	77.06
Oct	300	76.92
1932 – Jan	260	77.38

	DRACHMA TO £1	DRACHMA TO $1
1932 – Apr	450	123.29
1933 – Jan	600	179.57
1934 – Jan	600	120
1935 – Jan	516	104.67
1936 – Jan	520	109
1937 – Jan	550	111
1938 – Jan	550	113
1939 – Jan	550	125
1940 – Jan	535	151
1946 – Jan	20,000	5020 *Official*
	This continued to be the official rate although the un-official rate rose to about 42,000 to £1 and 15,000 to $1. This was made official in	
1951 – Jun	42,000	15,000
	This continued until a new official rate	
1953 – Jan	84,000	30,000
	Drachma revalued	
1954 – May	84	30
1955 – average	84	30
1956 – average	84	30
1957 – average	84	30
1958 – average	84	30
1959 – average	84	30
1960 – average	84	30
1961 – average	84	30
1962 – average	84	30
1963 – average	84	30
1964 – average	84	30
1965 – average	84	30
1966 – average	84	30
1967 – Jan	84	30
Nov	72	30
1968 – average	72	30
1969 – average	72	30

HUNGARY

1919 100 filler – 1 korona

	KORONA TO £1	KORONA TO $1
1919 – parity	24.02	4.93
1920 – Jan	611 – 835	165 – 222
Jun	650	165
Oct	1130 – 1540	330 – 420
1921 – Jan	1920 – 2170	495 – 570
Mar	1275 – 1717	310 – 410
Jun	910 – 975	220 – 260
Sep	1477 – 2710	395 – 725
Oct	2680 – 3150	715 – 797
1922 – Jan	2557 – 3300	605 – 750
Jun	3680 – 4435	826 – 1000
Sep	9150 – 11,250	2025 – 2537
1923 – Jan	10,250 – 14,000	2200 – 3010
Mar	13,000 – 22,000	2800 – 4700
Jun	22,000 – 43,000	4700 – 9400
Jul	35,000 – 100,000	7520 – 21,500
Nov	75,000 – 95,000	17,440 – 22,000
1924 – Jan	80,000 – 130,000	18,800 – 30,600
Apr	280,000 – 350,000	64,370 – 80,460
Oct	345,000	78,180
1925 – Jan	345,000	72,780

New currency introduced — 100 filler – 1 pengo

	PENGO TO £1	PENGO TO $1
1926 – Jan	27.7	5.72
1927 – Jan	27.7	5.72
1928 – Jan	27.9	5.72
1929 – Jan	27.8	5.72
1930 – Jan	27.8	5.72
1931 – Jan	27.8	5.72

	PENGO TO £1	PENGO TO $1
1932 – Jan	30	5.73
Sep	20	5.56
1933 – Jan	20	5.95
1934 – Jan	18.5	3.6
1935 – Jan	17	3.44
1936 – Jan	16.5	3.39
1937 – Jan	16.5	3.39
1938 – Jan	25	3.40
1939 – Jan	24	3.56
1940 – Jan	22	3.49
1946 – Jan	–	104,000
Apr	–	10.3 million
Jul	–	1,835 billion

At the end of July 1946 the pengo was replaced by the forint of 100 filler. The forint was worth 400,000,000,000,000,000,000,000,000,000 pengo. After this currency reform the official exchange rate was

	FORINT TO £1	FORINT TO $1
	32	11.7
until		
1967 – Nov	28.18	11.7

although more than double was usually given for Travellers' Cheques and in some other transactions

ITALY

100 centesimi – 1 lira

	LIRAS TO £1	LIRAS TO $1
1870	25.221	5.138
1914	25.3	5.2
1915 – Jan	25.89	5.33
Jun	28	5.85
1916 – Jan	32	6.69
1917 – Jan	34.65	7.30
Oct	37	7.77
1918 – Jan	40	8.42
Jun	44.1	9.1
1919 – Jan	30.3	6.33
Jun	37.33	8.05
Oct	41	9.81
1920 – Jan	50.4	13.63
Mar	63	18.54
Apr	102.5	25.62
Jun	66.45	17.0
Sep	81	22.95
1921 – Jan	102.86	29.05
Apr	95.82	24.30
Jun	73.5	18.77
Oct	93.58	25.14
1922 – Jan	98	23.20
Mar	83	18.6
Jun	90	20.25
Sep	102.5	22.91
1923 – Jan	95	20.43
Jul	105	22.58
1924 – Jan	97	22.82
Jul	101	23.22

	LIRAS TO £1	LIRAS TO $1
1925 – Jan	112.3	23.69
Jun	127	26.13
1926 – Jan	120	24.69
Aug	144	29.63
Nov	112	23.05
1927 – Jan	109.5	22.53
May	91	18.72
1928 – Jan	92.3	19
1929 – Jan	92.7	19
1930 – Jan	93.2	19
1931 – Jan	92.73	19
Oct	77	19.74
1932 – Jan	66.5	19.79
1933 – Jan	65.5	19.79
1934 – Jan	62	12.4
1935 – Jan	57	12.1
1936 – Jan	61.5	12.4
Oct		*Devaluation*
1937 – Jan	93.25	19
1938 – Jan	95	19
1939 – Jan	88	19.23
1940 – Jan	78	19.8

After the Allied invasion in 1943 the official rate was 400 lira to £1 and 100 lira to $1. The black market rate was often over 1000 to £1 and 250 to $1. The rate was officially stablized in

	LIRAS TO £1	LIRAS TO $1
1946 – Feb	900	225
1947 – Aug	1400	350
Dec	1961	589
1948 – Jan	2100	576
1949 – Jan	2317	575
Oct	1755	625
1950 – average	1740	625

	LIRAS TO £1	LIRAS TO $1
1951 – average	1750	625
1952 – average	1750	625
1953 – average	1750	625
1954 – average	1750	625
1955 – average	1750	625
1956 – average	1751	625
1957 – average	1751	625
1958 – average	1742	624
1959 – average	1742	620
1960 – average	1742	620
1961 – average	1742	620
1962 – average	1742	620
1963 – average	1742	622
1964 – average	1742	624
1965 – average	1742	624
1966 – average	1742	624
1967 – Jan	1740	624
Nov	1505	623
1968 – average	1500	623
1969 – average	1487	624

THE NETHERLANDS

100 cents – 1 gulder or florin

	FLORINS TO £1	FLORINS TO $1
1870	12.107	2.489
1914 – Jan	12.10	2.48
1915 – Jan	12.10	2.48
1916 – Jan	11	2.30
1917 – Jan	11.70	2.45
1918 – Jan	11	2.31
1919 – Jan	11.25	2.36
1920 – Jan	10	2.67
1921 – Jan	11.4	2.94
1922 – Jan	11.5	2.6
1923 – Jan	11.7	2.52
1924 – Jan	11.3	2.66
1925 – Jan	11.71	2.47
1926 – Jan	12.04	2.48
1927 – Jan	12.12	2.49
1928 – Jan	12.1	2.49
1929 – Jan	12	2.49
1930 – Jan	12	2.49
1931 – Jan	12	2.49
Oct	9.75	2.49
1932 – Jan	8.4	2.50
1933 – Jan	8.35	2.49
1934 – Jan	8	1.6
1935 – Jan	7.25	1.57
1936 – Jan	7.25	1.57
1937 – Jan	9	1.82
1938 – Jan	9	1.82
1939 – Jan	8.5	1.88
1940 – Jan	7.5	1.88

	FLORINS TO £1	FLORINS TO $1
1946 – average	10.69	2.66
1947 – average	10.69	2.66
1948 – average	10.69	2.66
1949 – Jan	10.64	2.65
Oct	10.64	3.8 *Devalued*
1950 – average	10.60	3.8
1951 – average	10.60	3.8
1952 – average	10.60	3.8
1953 – average	10.59	3.8
1954 – average	10.63	3.8
1955 – average	10.62	3.8
1956 – average	10.64	3.8
1957 – average	10.64	3.78
1958 – average	10.59	3.77
1959 – average	10.60	3.77
1960 – average	10.59	3.77
1961 – Mar	10.08	3.6
1962 – average	10.12	3.6
1963 – average	10.08	3.6
1964 – average	10.08	3.6
1965 – average	10.08	3.6
1966 – average	10.11	3.6
1967 – Jan	10.05	3.6
Nov	8.68	3.6
1968 – average	8.65	3.6
1969 – average	8.6	3.62

NORWAY

From 1876   100 ore – 1 krone

	KRONE TO £1	KRONE TO $1
Pre-war parity	18.16	3.73
1915 – Jan	19.33	4.0
1916 – Jan	17.5	3.74
1917 – Jan	17.1	3.61
1918 – Jan	14.95	3.13
1919 – Jan	17	3.57
1920 – Jan	19	5.02
1921 – Jan	21	5.46
Oct	30	7.60
1922 – Jan	27	6.4
1923 – Jan	25	5.38
1924 – Jan	30	7.06
1925 – Jan	31.3	6.60
Oct	24	4.94
1926 – Jan	23.8	4.9
1927 – Jan	19.0	3.91
1928 – Jan	18.3	3.77
1929 – Jan	18.2	3.73
1930 – Jan	18.2	3.73
1931 – Jan	18.2	3.73
Oct	18.	4.62
1932 – Jan	18.2	5.42
1933 – Jan	19.4	5.77
1934 – Jan	19.9	4.98
1935 – Jan	19.9	4.03
1936 – Jan	19.9	4.03
1937 – Jan	19.9	4.04
1938 – Jan	19.9	4.09
1939 – Jan	19.9	4.32

	KRONE TO £1	KRONE TO $1
1940 – Jan	17.7	4.40
1945 – average	20	4.77
1946 – average	20	4.97
1947 – average	20	4.97
1948 – average	20	4.97
1949 – Jan	20	4.96
Oct	20	7.14 *Devalued*
1950 – average	20	7.14
1951 – average	20	7.14
1952 – average	19.99	7.15
1953 – average	19.99	7.15
1954 – average	20.01	7.14
1955 – average	20.01	7.14
1956 – average	19.99	7.15
1957 – average	19.99	7.14
1958 – average	20.01	7.15
1959 – average	20.02	7.15
1960 – average	20.03	7.15
1961 – average	20.01	7.15
1962 – average	20.04	7.15
1963 – average	20.04	7.15
1964 – average	19.98	7.15
1965 – average	19.98	7.15
1966 – average	19.98	7.15
1967 – Jan	19.98	7.15
Nov	17.24	7.15
1968 – average	17.14	7.15
1969 – average	17.0	7.14

POLAND

1919 100 fenigi – 1 mark

	MARK TO £1	MARK TO $1
1919 – official parity	20.429	4.198
1920 – Jan	380 – 580	102 – 156
May	720 – 800	187 – 207
Oct	900 – 1100	260 – 319
Dec	1750 – 2320	500 – 660
1921 – Jan	2320 – 3600	650 – 950
May	3410 – 4100	833 – 1020
Sep	11,000 – 24,500	3100 – 7000
Nov	10,300 – 15,300	2625 – 4050
1922 – Jan	13,400	3120
Mar	18,100	4110
Jul	21,475 – 27,150	4850 – 6070
Aug	26,850 – 38,600	6045 – 8600
Oct	38,950 – 62,800	8925 – 14,125
Dec	78,150 – 82,550	17,275 – 17,700
1923 – Jan	80,000 – 160,000	17,200 – 34,400
Mar	320,000 – 345,000	68,000 – 73,400
Jul	475,000 – 1,000,000	105,500 – 222,000
Oct	1,600.000 – 8,500,000	355,000 – 1,888,000
Dec	15,000,000 – 27,000,000	3,450,000 – 6,200,000
1924 – Jan	25,500,000 – 42,000,000	6,000,000 – 9,880,000
May	40,000,000 – 45,000,000	9,000,000 – 10,300,000

1924 – Jun *New currency introduced — 100 groszy – 1 zloty*

	ZLOTY TO £1	ZLOTY TO $1
1924 – Jul	22.5	5.29
1925 – Jan	24.6	5.19
Nov	31	6.38
1926 – Jan	43	8.85
1927 – Jan	43.5	8.95

	ZLOTY TO £1	ZLOTY TO $1
1928 – Jan	43.5	8.95
1929 – Jan	43.25	8.91
1930 – Jan	43.5	8.95
1931 – Jan	43.5	8.95
Oct	35	8.98
1932 – Jan	30	8.93
1933 – Jan	30	8.93
1934 – Jan	29	5.8
1935 – Jan	26	5.30
1936 – Jan	26	5.30
1937 – Jan	26	5.28
1938 – Jan	26	5.30
1939 – Jan	24.5	5.30
1946 – Apr	403	100
1950 – Jan	1120	400
A new zloty was then introduced		
1950 – Oct	11.17	3.99
Various other rates were introduced: for example		
1957 – Feb	67	24 *(Tourists)*
but it continued the official rate until		
1967 – Nov	9.6	4
making the tourist rate		
	57	24

PORTUGAL

1000 reis – 1 milreis. In 1870 there were 4.1 milreis to £1 and .9 to $1. Subsequently the main coinage was 100 centavos – 1 escudo

	ESCUDO TO £1	ESCUDO TO $1
Pre-war parity	5.4	1.1
1914 – Aug	6	1.24
1915 – Jan	6.8	1.41
1916 – Jan	7	1.48
1917 – Jan	7.9	1.63
1918 – Jan	8	1.68
1919 – Jan	6.8	1.44
Nov	10	2.43
1920 – Jan	12	3.34
Jun	20	5.10
Oct	24	7.02
1921 – Jan	40	10.75
Mar	48	12.26
Jun	30	7.98
Oct	40	10.40
1922 – Jan	60	14.20
Jun	60	13.50
Oct	80	17.90
1923 – Jan	96	20.67
1924 – Jan	120	28.24
1925 – Jan	96	20.25
1926 – Jan	96	19.75
1927 – Jan	96	19.75
1928 – Jan	96	19.75
1929 – Jan	109	22.6
1930 – Jan	108	22.22
1931 – Jan	108	22.22

	ESCUDO TO £1	ESCUDO TO $1
1931 – Oct	110	28.21
1932 – Jan	110	32.74
1933 – Jan	110	32.74
1934 – Jan	110	22
1935 – Jan	110	22.17
1936 – Jan	110	22.17
1937 – Jan	110	22.29
1938 – Jan	110	22.55
1939 – Jan	110	24.95
1940 – Jan	108	27.56
1946 – average	100	24.94
1947 – average	100	25
1948 – average	100	25
1949 – Jan	100	25
Oct	80.5	28.95
1950 – average	80.5	28.95
1951 – average	80.5	28.95
1952 – average	80.5	28.95
1953 – average	80.1	28.95
1954 – average	80.0	28.95
1955 – average	80.1	28.95
1956 – average	80.1	28.95
1957 – average	80.0	28.95
1958 – average	80.1	28.95
1959 – average	80.2	28.95
1960 – average	80.2	28.95
1961 – average	80.2	28.8
1962 – average	80.2	28.8
1963 – average	80.2	28.8
1964 – average	80.2	28.8
1965 – average	80.2	28.8
1966 – average	80.15	28.8

	ESCUDO TO £1	ESCUDO TO $1
1967 – Jan	80.2	28.8
Nov	69.44	28.8
1968 – average	68.5	28.8
1969 – average	68.0	28.8

ROUMANIA

100 bani – 1 leu

	LEI TO £1	LEI TO $1
Pre-war parity	25.222	5.183
1919 – Nov	94 – 140	
1920 – Jan	151 – 205	35 – 57
Mar	265 – 290	63.5 – 69.0
Jun	165 – 185	39.5 – 46.6
Oct	165 – 185	46.0 – 57.5
1921 – Jan	285	76.5
Jun	227 – 237	57.9 – 63.8
Oct	390 – 565	109.0 – 152.5
1922 – Jan	535 – 610	129 – 144
Mar	584 – 635	133 – 145
Jun	660 – 787	148 – 176
Oct	695 – 743	157 – 163
1923 – Jan	775 – 1290	166.7 – 277.4
Jun	865 – 950	186.0 – 204.3
1924 – Jan	830 – 880	195.3 – 207.0
Jun	970 – 1050	224.5 – 243.0
1925 – Jan	930	196.2
Jun	1017 – 1065	209.2 – 219.1
1926 – Jan	1050	216
1927 – Jan	925	190.32
1928 – Jan	788	162.14
1929 – Jan	805	167.18
1930 – Jan	818	168.31
1931 – Jan	817	168.31
Oct	660	169.23
1932 – Jan	560	166.67
1933 – Jan	570	169.64
1934 – Jan	545	109

	LEI TO £1	LEI TO $1
1935 – Jan	485	98.38
Aug	625	126.77
1936 – Jan	665	141.26
1937 – Jan	670	140.78
1938 – Jan	675	140.12
1939 – Jan	660	143.49
1947 – Feb	–	150,195
Mar	–	225,195
Jun	–	650,188
New lei were then introduced		
1947 – Aug	605	150
This continued until		
1949 – Oct	420	150
The leu was then linked to the rouble and revalued		
1952 – Feb	31.04	11.2
The leu was again revalued		
1954 – Feb	16.8	6
Special rates were introduced: for example		
1957 – Jul	50.4	18 *(Tourists)*
These continued until		
1967 – Nov	14.4	6 *(Official)*
	28.8	12 *(Non-commercial)*
	43.2	16 *(Tourist)*

RUSSIA

100 kopeck – 1 rouble

	ROUBLES TO £1	ROUBLES TO $1
1870	6.3	
Pre-war parity	9.45	1.93
1915 – average	9.43	1.95
1916 – Jan	16	3.36
1917 – Jan	16.2	3.37

After the Revolution it is impossible to quote a rate that means anything. Gold 10 roubles and paper roubles were both circulating but in October 1923 the gold 10 roubles was worth 6,555,000,000 paper roubles. In December 1922 the Soviet Government introduced the chervonetz (equivalent to 10 gold roubles) with a parity value of £1.057 and $5.14. Subsequently the following rates were quoted but they bear no relation to the purchasing power of the respective currencies

1928 – Jan	9.46	1.94
1929 – Jan	9.42	1.94
1930 – Jan	9.48	1.94
1931 – Jan	9.42	1.94
Oct	7.4	1.9
1932 – Jan	6.5	1.93
1933 – Jan	6.5	1.93
1934 – Jan	6.3	1.93
1935 – Jan	5.7	1.16
1936 – Jan	5.7	1.16
Apr	24.75	4.96 *(linked with franc)*
1937 – Jan	24.75	5.04
1938 – Jan	29.5	5.90

	ROUBLES TO £1	ROUBLES TO $1
1939 – Jan	24.5	5.29
1945 – onwards	14.84	5.3
1950 – Feb	11.2	4
1961 – Jan	2.52	.9
1969 – Jan	2.16	.9

SPAIN

100 centavos – 1 peseta
(Before the mid 1870s escudos, reals and cuartos were also circulating)

	PESETAS TO £1	PESETAS TO $1
1878	25.221	5.183
Pre-war parity	25.22	5.18
1914 – Jan	26.7	5.49
1915 – Jan	25.45	5.24
1916 – Jan	25.15	5.33
1917 – Jan	22.4	4.70
1918 – Jan	19.7	4.14
1919 – Jan	23.6	4.96
1920 – Jan	19.5	5.27
Jun	23.9	6.05
1921 – Jan	27.8	7.43
1922 – Jan	28.2	6.69
1923 – Jan	29.7	6.39
1924 – Jan	33.5	7.88
1925 – Jan	33.9	7.15
1926 – Jan	34.3	7.06
1927 – Jan	31.25	6.43
1928 – Jan	28.3	5.82
1929 – Jan	29.7	6.81
May	33.8	6.95
1930 – Jan	36.6	7.53
Aug	43.64	8.98
1931 – Jan	46.3	9.53
Oct	44	11.28
1932 – Jan	40	11.9
1933 – Jan	41	11.9
1934 – Jan	39.5	7.8

	PESETAS TO £1	PESETAS TO $1
1935 – Jan	36	7.46
1936 – Jan	36	7.46
1937 – Jan	–	– *Civil War*
1939 – Jan	–	– *Civil War*
1940 – Jan	39	11.69
1946 – Apr	44.13	11.95 *Official*
Subsequently differential rates were introduced, varying according to the type of transaction		
1948 – Dec	50.73 – 88.26	13.59 – 22.5
1949 – Jan	100	25 *Tourist Rate*
These multiple rates were abolished and a single rate instituted		
1957 – Apr	117	38.95
1959 – Jul	168	60.15 *Devalued*
1960 – average	168	60
1961 – average	168	60
1962 – average	167	59.97
1963 – average	167	59.96
1964 – average	167	59.95
1965 – average	167	59.99
1966 – average	166	60
1967 – Jan	166	60
Nov	166	69.7 *Devalued*
1968 – average	166	69.78
1969 – average	167	69.9

SWEDEN

100 ore – 1 krona
(Often called Rix dollar in the earlier part of the period)

	KRONA TO £1	KRONA TO $1
1870	18.16	3.73
1914 – Jan	18.24	3.75
1915 – Jan	19.25	3.99
1916 – Jan	17.2	3.61
1917 – Jan	16.1	3.43
1918 – Jan	14.3	3.05
1919 – Jan	16.6	3.49
1920 – Jan	17.8	4.76
1921 – Jan	17.5	4.60
1922 – Jan	17	4.09
1923 – Jan	17.3	3.72
1924 – Jan	16.3	3.84
1925 – Jan	17.6	3.71
1926 – Jan	18	3.72
1927 – Jan	18.1	3.73
1928 – Jan	18.1	3.73
1929 – Jan	18.1	3.73
1930 – Jan	18.1	3.73
1931 – Jan	18.1	3.73
Oct	17	4.36
1932 – Jan	17.7	5.37
1933 – Jan	18.3	5.45
1934 – Jan	19.4	3.88
1935 – Jan	19.4	3.91
1936 – Jan	19.4	3.91
1937 – Jan	19.4	3.92
1938 – Jan	19.4	3.98
1939 – Jan	19.4	4.16

	KRONA TO £1	KRONA TO $1
1940 – Jan	18.9	4.20
1941 – average	16.9	4.20
1942 – average	16.9	4.20
1943 – average	16.9	4.20
1944 – average	16.9	4.20
1945 – average	16.9	4.20
1946 – average	15.77	3.92
1947 – average	14.49	3.6
1948 – average	14.49	3.6
1949 – Jan	14.49	3.6
Oct	14.49	5.18 *Devalued*
1950 – average	14.49	5.17
1951 – average	14.49	5.18
1952 – average	14.49	5.18
1953 – average	14.52	5.18
1954 – average	14.52	5.18
1955 – average	14.49	5.18
1956 – average	14.49	5.18
1957 – average	14.49	5.18
1958 – average	14.49	5.18
1959 – average	14.51	5.18
1960 – average	14.51	5.18
1961 – average	14.48	5.18
1962 – average	14.48	5.2
1963 – average	14.53	5.2
1964 – average	14.4	5.15
1965 – average	14.4	5.18
1966 – average	14.4	5.18
1967 – Jan	14.4	5.18
Nov	12.48	5.18
1968 – average	12.4	5.18
1969 – average	12.3	5.18

SWITZERLAND

100 centimes – 1 franc

	FRANCS TO £1		FRANCS TO $1
1870	25.2		5.183
1914 – Jan	25.18		5.18
1915 – Jan	25.57		5.28
1916 – Jan	24.90		5.23
1917 – Jan	23.92		5.02
1918 – Jan	21		4.42
1919 – Jan	23		4.82
1920 – Jan	21		5.62
1921 – Jan	24		6.40
1922 – Jan	21.75		5.16
1923 – Jan	25		5.38
1924 – Jan	24.5		5.76
1925 – Jan	24.3		5.13
1926 – Jan	25		5.14
1927 – Jan	25.1		5.14
1928 – Jan	25.27		5.2
1929 – Jan	25.2		5.18
1930 – Jan	25.13		5.16
1931 – Jan	25		5.14
Oct	20		5.13
1932 – Jan	17		5.05
1933 – Jan	17.4		5.18
1934 – Jan	16.7		3.34
1935 – Jan	15		3.04
1936 – Jan	15.2		3.05
Sep	21.4	*Devaluation*	4.34
1937 – Jan	21.3		4.35
1938 – Jan	21.6		4.38
1939 – Jan	20.5		4.38

	FRANCS TO £1	FRANCS TO $1
1940 – Jan	17.9	4.3
1941 – average	17.35	4.3
1942 – average	17.35	4.29
1943 – average	17.35	4.29
1944 – average	17.35	4.29
1945 – average	17.35	4.28
1946 – average	17.35	4.27
1947 – average	17.35	4.3
1948 – average	17.35	4.3
1949 – Jan	17.35	4.3
Oct	12.25	4.3
1950 – average	12.25	4.29
1951 – average	12.24	4.37
1952 – average	12.20	4.29
1953 – average	12.19	4.29
1954 – average	12.22	4.28
1955 – average	12.23	4.28
1956 – average	12.23	4.28
1957 – average	12.23	4.28
1958 – average	12.23	4.30
1959 – average	12.14	4.32
1960 – average	12.13	4.30
1961 – average	12.10	4.32
1962 – average	12.14	4.32
1963 – average	12.10	4.32
1964 – average	12.06	4.32
1965 – average	12.10	4.32
1966 – average	12.08	4.32
1967 – Jan	12.08	4.30
Nov	10.42	4.30
1968 – average	10.3	4.30
1969 – average	10.2	4.32

TURKEY

100 piastres or kurus – 1 Turkish pound or lira
(The Turkish pound was often called a medjidie in the early part of the period)

	LIRAS TO £1	LIRAS TO $1
Pre-war parity	1.1	4.39
1921 – Jan	5.7	1.50
Jun	5.2	1.37
Oct	6.8	1.79
1922 – Jan	6.95	1.65
1923 – Jan	8.1	1.74
1924 – Jan	8.6	2.02
1925 – Jan	8.2	1.73
1926 – Jan	9.6	1.97
1927 – Jan	9.6	1.97
1928 – Jan	9.4	1.95
1929 – Jan	10	2.07
1930 – Jan	10.45	2.15
1931 – Jan	10.25	2.15
Nov	7.7	2.08
1932 – Jan	7.0 – 7.5	2.08 – 2.23
1933 – Jan	6.98	2.06
1934 – Jan	6.7	1.34
1935 – Jan	6.06	1.24
1936 – Jan	6.2	1.26
1937 – Jan	6.13	1.26
1938 – Jan	6.2	1.25
1939 – Jan	5.75	1.28
1940 – Jan	5.21	1.38
1941 – Jan	–	1.31
1942 – Jan	–	1.31

		LIRAS TO £1	LIRAS TO $1
1943 –	Jan	–	1.31
1944 –	Jan	–	1.31
1945 –	Jan	–	1.30
1946 –	Jan	–	1.82
	Sep	11.28	2.83
	These continued the official rates until		
1949 –	Nov	7.84	2.83
	Then numerous different rates were introduced – one rate covered export of opium, tobacco and copper while another covered raisins, figs and hazel nuts. There was another rate for tourists. Various premiums brought the rate up to		
1958 –	Aug	25.2	9
	This became the sole rate in		
1960 –	Aug	25.32	9
	and continued until		
1967 –	Nov	21.6	9
	Subsequently a new tourist rate was introduced		
1968 –	average	28.8	12

YUGOSLAVIA

100 paras – 1 dinar

	DINARS TO £1	DINARS TO $1
Official parity	25.22	5.183
1920 – Apr	155 – 180	41.0 – 44.5
May	108 – 166	28.0 – 41.0
Jul	60	16
Sep	96 – 105	26.5 – 29.0
1921 – Jan	138	35.6
Sep	160 – 225	45.2 – 60.2
Oct	215 – 302	57.3 – 75.0
1922 – Jan	286 – 323	70.5 – 75.0
Mar	335 – 362	77.0 – 82.0
Aug	370 – 388	81.0 – 86.5
Dec	326 – 429	72.0 – 92.8
1923 – Jan	420 – 650	90.3 – 139.8
Apr	430 – 470	92.5 – 101.0
Aug	410 – 450	89.7 – 97.4
1924 – Jan	360 – 400	84.7 – 94.1
Jun	352 – 385	81.5 – 89.1
Oct	315	70
1925 – Jan	267 – 308	56.3 – 65
Jun	282	58
Oct	273	56.4
1926 – Jan	275	56.6
1927 – Jan	275	56.6
1928 – Jan	276	56.85
1929 – Jan	276	56.85
1930 – Jan	275	56.6
1931 – Jan	274	56.5
Oct	220	56.4
1932 – Jan	190	56.5

	DINARS TO £1	DINARS TO $1
1933 – Jan	240	72.43
1934 – Jan	240	48.0
1935 – Jan	216	43.41
1936 – Jan	216	43.41
1937 – Jan	216	43.41
1938 – Jan	216	43.43
1939 – Jan	208	44.19
1940 – Jan	200	44.55
After the war the Government exercised strict control over foreign exchange. Different rates were given for different types of transactions. The official rate was		
1947	201	50
1948	201	50
1949 – Jan	201	50
Nov	140	50
This continued until an official devaluation		
1952 – Jan	840	300
From 1954 preferential rates were given for some purposes bringing the effective exchange rate to 1680 dinars to £1 and 632 to $1. A new rate was introduced		
1961 – Sep	2100	750
This lasted until a further devaluation		
1965 – Jul	3500	1250
New currency was introduced		
1966 – Jan	35	12.5
and has remained unchanged except		
1967 – Nov	30	12.5

JAPAN

100 sen – 1 yen

	YEN TO £1	YEN TO $1
Pre-1914	10	2
1915 – Jan	10	2
1916 – Jan	10	2
1917 – Jan	10	2
1918 – Jan	10	2
1919 – Jan	10	2
1920 – Jan	10	2
1921 – Jan	10	2
1922 – Jan	10	2
1923 – Jan	10	2.15
1924 – Jan	10	2.35
1925 – Jan	12	2.53
1926 – Jan	11.25	2.31
1927 – Jan	10	2.10
1928 – Jan	10.25	2.11
1929 – Jan	10.25	2
1930 – Jan	10	2
1931 – Jan	10	2
Oct	8	2.05
1932 – Jan	9.8	2.92
Sep	16	4.62
1933 – Jan	16.5	4.91
1934 – Jan	16.5	4.91
1935 – Jan	17	3.4
1936 – Jan	17	3.4
1937 – Jan	17	3.4
1938 – Jan	17	3.5
1939 – Jan	17	3.84
1940 – Jan	17	4.26

	YEN TO £1	YEN TO $1
1945	–	15 *Military rate*
1947 – Mar	–	50
1948 – Jul	–	270
1949 – Apr	1480	360
Nov	1010	360
1950 – average	1010	360
1951 – average	1010	360
1952 – average	1010	360
1953 – average	1010	360
1954 – average	1011	360
1955 – average	1011	360
1956 – average	1005	360
1957 – average	1012	360
1958 – average	1010	360
1959 – average	1007	360
1960 – average	1008	360
1961 – average	1016	360
1962 – average	1007	360
1963 – average	1013	360
1964 – average	1001	360
1965 – average	1013	360
1966 – average	1012	360
1967 – Jan	1012	360
Nov	864	360
1968 – average	860	360
1969 – average	858	360

ARGENTINA

100 centavos – 1 peso

	PESO TO £1	PESO TO $1
Pre-war parity	5	1.06
1917 – Jan	4.9	1.00
1918 – Jan	4.9	1.00
1919 – Jan	4.8	.99
1920 – Jan	4	1.03
1921 – Jan	4.8	1.28
1922 – Jan	5.8	1.28
1923 – Jan	5.8	1.25
1924 – Jan	6.0	1.41
1925 – Jan	5.5	1.16
1926 – Jan	5.5	1.13
1927 – Jan	5.5	1.13
1928 – Jan	5.2	1.08
1929 – Jan	5.1	1.03
In December 1929 Argentina went off the Gold Standard		
1930 – Jan	5.4	1.15
1931 – Jan	6.5	1.34
Exchange control was introduced in October 1931		
1932 – Jan	6	1.79
1933 – Jan	5.3	1.58
From November 1933 there were 'free' and 'official' rates of exchange in operation. It is therefore impossible to quote an exact rate of what the peso was worth. Subsequent figures are in 'paper' pesos as compared with the previous ones which were in 'gold' pesos. A 'gold' peso equalled 2.2727 'paper' pesos		
1934 – Jan	17	3.4
1935 – Jan	19	3.85
1936 – Jan	17	3.59

	PESO TO £1	PESO TO $1
1937 – Jan	16	3.33
1938 – Jan	17	3.92
1939 – Jan	17	3.27
1940 – average	17	4.37
1941 – average	17	4.24
1942 – average	17	4.23
1943 – average	17	4.06
1944 – average	17	3.98
1945 – average	17	3.98
1946 – average	17	3.98
1947 – average	17	4.08
1948 – Jun	19.4	4.8

In October 1949 the official rate of exchange was established at 7.2 pesos to $1. This was raised to 7.5 in January 1951 and to 18 in 1955. There were, however, at times (e.g. in December 1949) ten different rates of exchange varying from 3.36 pesos to 15.8 pesos to $1. Figures quoted for this period are therefore meaningless. A free rate was allowed in

1959 – Jan	196	68.8
Jun	241	85.7
1960 – average	233	83
1961 – average	233	83
1962 – Jan	233	83
Apr	379	135
1963 – Jan	375	134
Sep	419	149
1964 – Jan	369	132
Oct	402	144
1965 – Jan	418	150
May	479	171
Oct	506	180
1966 – Jan	530	189

	PESO TO £1	PESO TO $1
1966 – May	565	202
Aug	601	215
1967 – Jan	685	245
Mar	979	350
Nov	840	350
1968 – average	836	350
1969 – average	836	350

BRAZIL

1000 reis – 100 centavos – 1 milreis

	MILREIS TO £1	MILREIS TO $1
Pre-war parity	15	3.080
1915 – Jan	17.75	3.17
1916 – Jan	20	4.04
1917 – Jan	20	4.27
1918 – Jan	17.75	3.72
1919 – Jan	18.5	3.92
1920 – Jan	13.75	3.72
1921 – Jan	25.25	6.78
1922 – Jan	32	7.87
1923 – Jan	40	8.60
1924 – Jan	40	9.41
1925 – Jan	40	8.44
1926 – Jan	34.25	6.64
1927 – Jan	41.75	8.6
1928 – Jan	40	8.23
1929 – Jan	40	8.36
1930 – Jan	43.5	8.95
1931 – Jan	53.3	10.97
In May 1931 exchange control was introduced, with certain transactions at official rates and others at free rates. All subsequent figures for Brazil are approximate		
1931 – Oct	80	20.51
1932 – Jan	60	17.86
1933 – Jan	43.5	12.95
1934 – Jan	60	16
1935 – Jan	84.9	17.22
1936 – average	86.3	17.33
1937 – average	79.6	16.08
1938 – average	83.5	18.17

	MILREIS TO £1	MILREIS TO $1
1939 – average	81.9	19.71
1940 – average	73.7	19.79

New currency: 100 centavos – 1 cruzeiro

	CRUZEIRO TO £1	CRUZEIRO TO $1
1942 – average	83.6	19.64
1943 – average	83.6	19.63
1944 – average	83.6	19.57
1945 – average	82.8	19.50
1946 – average	79	18.72
1947 – average	79	18.72
1948 – average	79	18.72
1949 – Oct	52	18.72

After 1949 for some years it is impossible to give a meaningful exchange rate. The official rate remained for some years at 18.72 to $1 while in 1954 the free rate was 180 cruzeiros to $1 at 120 days' delivery. In April 1963 official rates varied from 180 to 623 cruzeiros to $1. Official rates lagged far behind while free rates reached

1964 – Nov	4400	1610 *Standard rate*
Dec	5145	1850
1965 – Nov	6216	2220
1966 – average	6216	2220
1967 – Jan	6130	2200
Feb	7.7	2.7 *New cruzeiros*
Nov	6.5	2.7
1968 – Feb	7.6	3.2
Jun	7.6	3.2
1969 – Jan	9.0	3.5
Jun	9.6	4.0

MEXICO

100 centavos – 1 peso

	PESO TO £1	PESO TO $1
Pre-war parity	10	2
1919 – Jan	9	1.9
1920 – Jan	7.5	1.8
1921 – Jan	7.75	2
1922 – Jan	8.5	2.1
1923 – Jan	8.3	1.78
1924 – Jan	9	2.12
1925 – Jan	8	1.69
1926 – Jan	10	2
1927 – Jan	10	2
1928 – Jan	10	2
1929 – Jan	10	2
1930 – Jan	10	2
1931 – Jan	10.2	2.1
1932 – Jan	8.5	2.53
1933 – Jan	10.5	3.6
Jun	15	3.7
1934 – Jan	18	3.6
1935 – Jan	18	3.6
1936 – Jan	18	3.6
1937 – Jan	18	3.6
1938 – Jan	18	4.5
1939 – Jan	*Not quoted*	5.18
1940 – Jan	*Not quoted*	5.18
1941 – average	20.5	4.86
1942 – average	20.5	4.86
1943 – average	20.5	4.86
1944 – average	20	4.86
1945 – average	20	4.86

	PESO TO £1	PESO TO $1
1946 – average	20	4.86
1947 – average	19.5	4.86
1948 – Aug	27	6.83
1949 – Jan	27	6.88
1950 – average	24.25	8.65
1951 – average	24.25	8.65
1952 – average	24.25	8.65
1953 – average	24.25	8.65
1954 – Apr	35	12.49
This continued the official rate until		
1967 – Nov	29.85	12.49
1968 – average	29.8	12.49
1969 – average	29.75	12.49

LONDON GOLD PRICES

Under the Bank Charter Act of 1844, the Bank of England was bound to buy and sell gold at the rate of 77 shillings and ninepence per ounce: the equivalent of 84 shillings and ninepence per fine ounce. The first figures, given in shillings and pence per ounce, are chosen at random to show how little the rate fluctuated before 1914

1870 – Mar	77	9
1879 – Jun	77	9
1887 – Oct	77	9
1898 – Aug	77	10
1900 – Jan	77	9
1902 – Jan	77	10
1904 – Jan	77	10
1906 – Aug	77	9
1908 – Jun	77	10
1909 – Jan	77	11
1910 – Jun	77	9
After the war when trading was resumed, figures were quoted in shillings and pence per ounce		
1920 – Jan	109	
Jun	103	2
1921 – Jan	115	10
Jun	108	2
1922 – Jan	97	9
Jun	91	9
1923 – Jan	88	11
Jun	89	4
1924 – Jan	95	8
Jun	84	11
1925 – Jan	87	9

In April 1925, Great Britain returned to the Gold Standard at the rate of 84 shillings and elevenpence per fine ounce

1925 – Jun	84	11
1926 – Jan	84	11
Jun	84	11
1927 – Jan	84	10
Jun	84	11
1928 – Jan	84	11
Jun	84	10
1929 – Jan	84	11
Jun	84	11
1930 – Jan	84	11
Jun	85	
1931 – Jan	85	1
Jun	84	11

In September 1931 Great Britain went off the Gold Standard. Within a few days the price was

1931 – Sep	100	
1932 – Jan	120	7
Jun	114	
1933 – Jan	123	8
Jun	122	1
1934 – Jan	127	
Jun	138	1
1935 – Jan	141	6
Jun	141	2
1936 – Jan	141	2
Jun	138	7
1937 – Jan	141	6
Jun	140	5
1938 – Jan	139	
Jun	140	
1939 – Jan	150	5

	Jun	148	6
1940 –	Jan	168	
	May	168	
	After the war there was an official price at which the Bank of England would buy gold		
1945 –	Jun	172	3
	This continued until		
1949 –	Sep	248	
	This continued until the free market was reopened		
1954 –	Mar	248	
	There were then minor fluctuations		
1960 –	Jan	250	9
	Jun	250	8
1961 –	Jan	254	11
	Jun	251	8
1962 –	Jan	250	3
	Jun	250	2
1963 –	Jan	250	2
	Jun	251	3
1964 –	Jan	250	9
	Jun	251	3
1965 –	Jan	252	
	Jun	251	6
1966 –	Jan	250	10
	Jun	252	2
1967 –	Jan	252	1
	Jun	252	1
	until Sterling devaluation		
	Nov	290	10
1968 –	Jan	292	
	Jun	343	8
1969 –	Jan	352	6
	Jun	350	